ENHANCING PERSONAL AND PROFESSIONAL PRODUCTIVITY

Foreword

Welcome to the course on Enhancing Personal and Professional Productivity! In today's fast-paced world, the ability to manage time effectively, stay organized, and maintain high levels of productivity is crucial for success both in our personal lives and careers. This course is designed for individuals eager to improve their productivity skills, optimize their workflow, and achieve greater efficiency in their daily tasks.

Throughout this course, you will explore practical strategies and techniques to boost your personal effectiveness and streamline your professional responsibilities. From mastering time management principles to adopting productivity tools and fostering a proactive mindset, you will learn how to maximize your potential and achieve your goals more effectively.

We will delve into topics such as goal setting, prioritization, overcoming procrastination, optimizing work environments, and leveraging technology for productivity gains. Whether you are seeking to enhance your individual performance or lead teams more effectively, this course will provide you with the knowledge and tools necessary to excel in today's competitive landscape.

Are you ready to embark on a journey towards enhancing your personal and professional productivity? Let's equip ourselves with the skills and strategies needed to thrive in our dynamic world!

Course: Enhancing Personal and Professional Productivity

Module 1: Introduction to Productivity _____ 5
1.1. What is Productivity and Why It Matters _____ 6
1.2. Core Principles of Productivity _____ 8
1.3. Self-Assessment of Current Productivity Level _____ 11

Module 2: Time Management _____ 13
2.1. Key Time Management Techniques _____ 14
2.2. Task Prioritization (ABC Method, Eisenhower Matrix) __ 16
2.3. Using Planners and Calendars _____ 18
2.4. Pomodoro Technique and GTD (Getting Things Done) _ 20

Module 3: Task and Project Management _____ 22
3.1. Setting SMART Goals _____ 23
3.2. Tools for Project Management (Trello, Asana) _____ 25
3.3. Delegation and Outsourcing _____ 28
3.4. Monitoring and Evaluating Progress _____ 31

Module 4: Personal Productivity _____ 33
4.1. Building Productive Habits _____ 34
4.2. Managing Energy and Health _____ 37
4.3. Minimizing Distractions _____ 40
4.4. Strategies to Enhance Focus _____ 42

Module 5: Professional Productivity _____ 45
5.1. Effective Communication at Work _____ 46
5.2. Teamwork and Leadership _____ 49
5.3. Managing Stress and Preventing Burnout _____ 52
5.4. Continuous Learning and Self-Development _____ 54

Module 6: Applying Knowledge in Practice _____ 57
6.1. Developing a Personal Productivity Plan _____ 58
6.2. Case Studies and Examples of Successful Individuals __ 61
6.3. Feedback and Plan Adjustments _____ 64

Additional Materials _____ 67
- Checklist _____ 68
- Recommended Books _____ 70

MODULE 1:
INTRODUCTION TO PRODUCTIVITY

1.1. What is Productivity and Why It Matters

What is Productivity?
Productivity refers to the efficiency with which tasks and goals are accomplished. It is not merely about getting things done, but about achieving meaningful outcomes with optimal effort and resources. In essence, productivity is the measure of output relative to input. High productivity means achieving better results in less time, with less effort.

Types of Productivity:
1. Personal Productivity: This involves managing your time, energy, and resources effectively to achieve personal goals and maintain a healthy work-life balance.
2. Professional Productivity: This pertains to your efficiency and effectiveness in the workplace, including how well you manage tasks, projects, and responsibilities to achieve career objectives.

Why Productivity Matters:
- Achieving Goals:

Productivity enables you to set and achieve both short-term and long-term goals more efficiently. It helps in breaking down large objectives into manageable tasks and ensures steady progress.
- Work-Life Balance:

Being productive allows you to complete work tasks efficiently, leaving more time for personal interests, family, and relaxation. This balance is crucial for overall well-being and long-term success.
- Stress Reduction:

Effective productivity strategies can reduce the feeling of being overwhelmed by tasks. By managing time and resources better, you can decrease stress and avoid burnout.

- Career Advancement:

High productivity at work can lead to recognition, promotions, and greater career opportunities. Employers value employees who can deliver results efficiently and effectively.

- Improved Quality of Work:

When you are productive, you can focus more on the quality of your work rather than just the quantity. This leads to better outcomes, increased satisfaction, and a sense of accomplishment.

- Resource Management:

Productivity involves making the best use of available resources, including time, energy, and materials. This not only saves costs but also promotes sustainable practices.

The Importance of Measuring Productivity:

To enhance productivity, it is essential to measure and track it regularly. This helps in identifying areas for improvement and implementing strategies to optimize performance. Common metrics for measuring productivity include:

- Time Tracking: Monitoring how much time is spent on various tasks and projects.
- Output Measurement: Assessing the quantity and quality of work produced.
- Goal Achievement: Tracking progress towards set goals and objectives.

In conclusion, productivity is a critical aspect of personal and professional life. It is about making the most of your time and resources to achieve meaningful results. By understanding what productivity is and why it matters, you can begin to implement strategies to enhance your efficiency and effectiveness, leading to greater success and fulfillment.

1.2. Core Principles of Productivity

1. Set Clear Goals:
Having clear, specific, and achievable goals is the foundation of productivity. Goals provide direction and a sense of purpose. Use the SMART criteria (Specific, Measurable, Achievable, Relevant, Time-bound) to set effective goals.
2. Prioritize Tasks:
Not all tasks are created equal. Prioritize tasks based on their importance and urgency. Use tools like the Eisenhower Matrix to categorize tasks and focus on what truly matters.
3. Plan and Organize:
Planning is crucial for productivity. Create daily, weekly, and monthly plans to outline what needs to be done. Organize tasks using to-do lists, planners, or digital tools like Trello or Asana. This helps in managing time efficiently and reducing the likelihood of missing important deadlines.
4. Manage Time Effectively:
Time management is a key principle of productivity. Techniques such as the Pomodoro Technique (working in focused intervals with breaks) or time blocking (allocating specific time slots for different activities) can enhance time management. Avoid multitasking, as it can reduce efficiency and lead to errors.
5. Eliminate Distractions:
Identify and minimize distractions that hinder productivity. This could involve turning off notifications, creating a dedicated workspace, or setting boundaries with family and friends during work hours. Tools like website blockers can help maintain focus.
6. Take Regular Breaks:
Taking breaks is essential to maintain high levels of productivity. Regular breaks prevent burnout and keep the

mind fresh and focused. Short breaks during work sessions, as well as longer breaks to recharge, are both important.

7. Continuous Improvement:

Productivity is an ongoing process. Continuously assess and refine your productivity strategies. Reflect on what works well and what doesn't, and be willing to adapt and change. Seeking feedback and learning from others can also contribute to continuous improvement.

8. Delegate and Outsource:

Recognize tasks that can be delegated or outsourced. Delegating allows you to focus on high-priority tasks that require your expertise, while outsourcing can save time and resources. Trusting others to handle certain tasks can significantly boost overall productivity.

9. Maintain Work-Life Balance:

Balance between work and personal life is crucial for sustained productivity. Allocate time for hobbies, relaxation, and family. A well-balanced life enhances motivation and prevents burnout.

10. Use Technology Wisely:

Leverage productivity tools and technologies to streamline tasks. Calendar apps, task management software, and automation tools can save time and increase efficiency. However, be mindful of over-reliance on technology and ensure it complements your productivity strategies.

11. Stay Healthy:

Physical and mental health directly impact productivity. Maintain a healthy lifestyle with regular exercise, a balanced diet, and adequate sleep. Mental well-being can be supported through mindfulness practices, stress management techniques, and seeking professional help when needed.

By understanding and implementing these core principles, you can enhance your productivity in both personal and professional aspects of life. These principles serve as a guide to achieving better results with less effort and in a more efficient manner.

1.3. Self-Assessment of Current Productivity Level

Why Self-Assessment Matters:
Self-assessment is essential for understanding your current productivity level and identifying areas for improvement. It allows you to objectively evaluate how effectively you are managing your time, tasks, and goals.
Steps for Self-Assessment:
1. Reflect on Your Goals:
Review the goals you have set for yourself, both personally and professionally. Are you making progress towards them? Are they still relevant and achievable?
2. Analyze Your Time Management:
Assess how you currently manage your time. Do you prioritize tasks effectively? Are you spending time on activities that align with your goals?
3. Evaluate Your Task Management:
Consider how you organize and manage your tasks. Are you using tools and techniques to stay organized? Are there tasks that consistently get delayed or forgotten?
4. Reflect on Productive Habits:
Think about your daily habits and routines. Which habits contribute positively to your productivity? Are there habits or behaviors that are hindering your progress?
5. Assess Distraction Management:
Identify common distractions that impact your focus and productivity. How well do you manage these distractions? What strategies could help minimize their impact?
6. Review Work-Life Balance:
Evaluate how well you balance work responsibilities with personal life. Are you able to disconnect from work and recharge? Are there adjustments needed to achieve a healthier balance?

Tools for Self-Assessment:
- Productivity Metrics: Use tools or apps to track metrics such as task completion rates, time spent on specific activities, and goal progress.
- Feedback from Others: Seek input from colleagues, mentors, or friends who can provide constructive feedback on your productivity habits and effectiveness.

Benefits of Self-Assessment:
- Awareness: Gain clarity on your strengths and weaknesses related to productivity.
- Goal Setting: Use insights from self-assessment to set realistic and meaningful goals for improvement.
- Continuous Improvement: Take proactive steps to implement changes and enhance your productivity over time.
- Accountability: Hold yourself accountable for achieving productivity goals and maintaining consistent progress.

Conclusion:
Self-assessment is a valuable tool for anyone looking to improve their productivity. By regularly assessing your current practices and making adjustments where necessary, you can develop more effective habits, achieve your goals more efficiently, and lead a more balanced and fulfilling life.

MODULE 2:
TIME MANAGEMENT

2.1. Key Time Management Techniques

Effective time management is crucial for maximizing productivity and achieving goals. Here are some key techniques to help you manage your time more efficiently:

1. Prioritization:
Prioritize tasks based on their importance and urgency. Use methods like the ABC method (assigning priorities A, B, or C to tasks) or the Eisenhower Matrix (categorizing tasks into urgent, important, not urgent, and not important) to determine which tasks to tackle first.

2. Time Blocking:
Allocate specific time blocks for different tasks or activities throughout your day. This technique helps you focus on one task at a time and prevents multitasking, which can reduce efficiency.

3. Set SMART Goals:
SMART goals are Specific, Measurable, Achievable, Relevant, and Time-bound. Setting clear and specific goals helps you stay focused and motivated, leading to better time management and productivity.

4. Use a Planner or Calendar:
Use a physical planner or digital calendar to schedule tasks, appointments, and deadlines. Regularly reviewing your planner helps you stay organized and ensures you don't miss important commitments.

5. Pomodoro Technique:
The Pomodoro Technique involves working on a task for a set period (usually 25 minutes) followed by a short break (5 minutes). After completing four Pomodoro sessions, take a longer break (15-30 minutes). This method can improve focus and productivity by breaking tasks into manageable intervals.

6. Avoid Procrastination:
Procrastination can derail productivity. Identify tasks you

tend to procrastinate on and use strategies like setting deadlines, breaking tasks into smaller steps, or starting with the most challenging task first to overcome procrastination.

7. Batch Similar Tasks:

Group similar tasks together and complete them consecutively. This approach minimizes context switching and allows you to maintain focus on similar types of work.

8. Delegate Tasks:

Delegate tasks that others can handle effectively, freeing up your time for tasks that require your unique skills and expertise. Effective delegation is key to managing workload and improving overall productivity.

9. Review and Adjust:

Regularly review your time management strategies and adjust them as needed. Reflect on what is working well and what can be improved to optimize your productivity over time.

10. Limit Distractions:

Identify common distractions (e.g., social media, emails) and take steps to minimize their impact. This may include setting designated times for checking emails or using website blockers to avoid distractions during focused work sessions.

Implementing these time management techniques can help you make the most of your time, increase productivity, and achieve your goals more effectively. Tailor these techniques to fit your personal preferences and work style for optimal results.

2.2. Task Prioritization

Effective task prioritization is essential for managing your workload and maximizing productivity. Here are key methods and techniques for prioritizing tasks:

1. ABC Method:
   Assigning Priorities: Classify tasks into categories:
   - A tasks: High priority tasks that are urgent and important.
   - B tasks: Tasks that are important but not urgent.
   - C tasks: Tasks that are neither urgent nor important.

   Benefits: Helps you focus on completing high-priority tasks first, ensuring that critical deadlines are met and important goals are achieved.

2. Eisenhower Matrix:
   Categorizing Tasks:
   - Urgent and Important: Tasks that require immediate attention and are crucial to your goals.
   - Important but Not Urgent: Tasks that contribute to your long-term goals but can be scheduled for later.
   - Urgent but Not Important: Tasks that demand immediate action but do not contribute significantly to your goals.
   - Not Urgent and Not Important: Tasks that are time-wasters and should be minimized or eliminated.

   Benefits: Provides a visual framework for prioritizing tasks based on their urgency and importance, helping you allocate time and resources effectively.

3. Pareto Principle (80/20 Rule):
   Identifying Critical Tasks: Focus on the 20% of tasks that yield 80% of the results or impact. Identify tasks that contribute the most to your goals or outcomes.

   Benefits: Maximizes productivity by concentrating efforts on tasks that deliver significant results, rather than spreading

time and energy evenly across all tasks.

4. Value vs. Effort Analysis:
- Assessing Tasks: Evaluate tasks based on their value (impact on goals, outcomes) and effort required (time, resources). Prioritize tasks that offer high value relative to effort.
- Benefits: Ensures that your time is invested in tasks that align with your goals and deliver meaningful outcomes, optimizing productivity and efficiency.

5. Consider Deadlines and Dependencies:
- Time Sensitivity: Prioritize tasks with approaching deadlines or dependencies on other tasks or individuals. Ensure that critical tasks are completed on time to avoid delays and bottlenecks.
- Benefits: Helps you manage workload effectively by addressing time-sensitive tasks promptly and coordinating dependencies to maintain workflow continuity.

6. Continuous Review and Adjustment:
- Regular Assessment: Periodically review and reassess task priorities based on changes in deadlines, goals, or project requirements.
- Benefits: Allows flexibility to adapt priorities to evolving circumstances, ensuring that your time and efforts are consistently aligned with current objectives and priorities.

By applying these task prioritization techniques, you can enhance your time management skills, increase productivity, and achieve greater efficiency in both personal and professional endeavors. Tailor these methods to fit your specific needs and work environment for optimal results.

2.3. Using Planners and Calendars

Effectively utilizing planners and calendars is essential for organizing tasks, managing time, and improving productivity. Here's how to leverage these tools effectively:

1. Choose the Right Tool:

Select a planner or digital calendar that suits your preferences and workflow. Consider whether you prefer a physical planner for writing tasks by hand or a digital calendar for easy access and synchronization across devices.

2. Schedule Regular Planning Sessions:

Set aside dedicated time each day or week to plan and organize tasks. Use this time to review upcoming deadlines, prioritize tasks, and schedule activities in your planner or calendar.

3. Break Down Tasks:

Divide larger projects or goals into smaller, actionable tasks. Enter these tasks into your planner or calendar with specific deadlines or milestones to track progress and ensure completion.

4. Set Reminders and Alerts:

Utilize reminders and alerts to notify you of upcoming tasks, deadlines, or appointments. Set reminders in advance to allow sufficient preparation time and reduce last-minute rush.

5. Block Time for Focus and Concentration:

Implement time blocking techniques to allocate dedicated time slots for focused work on specific tasks or projects. Block off uninterrupted periods in your calendar to minimize distractions and maximize productivity.

6. Prioritize and Color-Code Tasks:

Use prioritization techniques (such as the ABC method or Eisenhower Matrix) to rank tasks by importance and urgency.

Color-code tasks or categories in your planner or calendar for visual clarity and quick reference.

7. Maintain Flexibility:

Allow flexibility in your schedule to accommodate unexpected tasks, changes in priorities, or unforeseen events. Leave buffer time between appointments or tasks to handle emergencies or additional work as needed.

8. Review and Adjust Regularly:

Periodically review your planner or calendar to assess progress, adjust priorities, and update tasks or deadlines as necessary. Reflect on what worked well and what can be improved to refine your time management strategies.

9. Integrate Personal and Professional Activities:

Consolidate personal and professional commitments in one unified planner or calendar. This holistic approach helps you maintain a balanced schedule and avoid conflicts between work and personal life.

10. Sync Across Devices:

If using a digital calendar, sync it across all your devices (computer, smartphone, tablet) to access your schedule anytime, anywhere. Ensure synchronization to stay updated with changes and maintain consistency in your planning.

11. Use Additional Features and Apps:

Explore additional features and apps that complement your planner or calendar, such as task management tools, note-taking apps, or productivity extensions. Integrate these tools to streamline workflow and enhance productivity.

By effectively utilizing planners and calendars, you can enhance your time management skills, improve organization, and increase productivity in both personal and professional aspects of life. Consistent use and proactive planning will help you stay focused, meet deadlines, and achieve your goals efficiently.

2.4. Pomodoro Technique

The Pomodoro Technique is a popular time management method that enhances focus and productivity by breaking work into intervals separated by short breaks. Here's how to implement the Pomodoro Technique effectively:

1. Work Interval (Pomodoro):
- Set a timer for a focused work interval, traditionally 25 minutes (one Pomodoro). During this time, concentrate solely on the task at hand without distractions.

2. Short Break:
- After completing a Pomodoro, take a short break of 5 minutes. Use this time to relax, stretch, or briefly step away from your workspace to refresh your mind.

3. Repeat and Long Break:
- After completing four Pomodoro sessions (approximately 2 hours), take a longer break of 15-30 minutes. This extended break allows for mental recharge before resuming work.

4. Benefits of the Pomodoro Technique:
- Enhanced Focus: By working in focused intervals, you can maintain concentration and avoid distractions that can disrupt productivity.
- Time Management: Breaking tasks into manageable intervals helps in prioritizing and completing tasks efficiently.
- Reduced Procrastination: The structured approach encourages getting started on tasks and maintaining momentum throughout the work session.
- Improved Work-Life Balance: Regular breaks prevent burnout and promote a healthier balance between work and personal life.

5. Adjusting Pomodoro Sessions:
- Customize the duration of Pomodoro sessions and breaks

based on your preference and work style. Some individuals may find shorter or longer intervals more suitable for their concentration levels.

6. Tools and Apps:
- Use timers or Pomodoro apps to automate intervals and breaks. These tools can track Pomodoro sessions, provide notifications for breaks, and maintain consistency in your time management practice.

7. Integrating with Task Management:
- Combine the Pomodoro Technique with task prioritization methods (e.g., ABC method, Eisenhower Matrix) to focus on high-priority tasks during Pomodoro sessions. Allocate Pomodoro sessions based on task importance and deadlines.

8. Overcoming Challenges:
- Address common challenges such as interruptions, fatigue, or difficulty maintaining focus by practicing mindfulness techniques, adjusting workspace environment, or using noise-canceling headphones.

9. Continuous Improvement:
- Reflect on your experience with the Pomodoro Technique and make adjustments to optimize productivity. Experiment with session lengths, break durations, and environmental factors to find what works best for you.

By incorporating the Pomodoro Technique into your time management routine, you can increase productivity, manage tasks effectively, and maintain focus throughout your workday. Regular practice and adaptation will help you achieve consistent results and accomplish your goals efficiently.

MODULE 3:
TASK AND PROJECT MANAGEMENT

3.1. Setting SMART Goals

Setting SMART goals is essential for effective task and project management. SMART is an acronym that stands for Specific, Measurable, Achievable, Relevant, and Time-bound. Here's how to set SMART goals:

1. Specific:
Clearly define the goal in detail. Specify what you want to achieve, why it is important, and who is involved. Avoid vague objectives and be precise in your description.
Example: Instead of "Increase sales," a specific goal would be "Increase quarterly sales revenue by 15% compared to last year."

2. Measurable:
Establish measurable criteria to track progress and determine when the goal is achieved. Quantify the goal with specific metrics, such as percentages, numbers, or deadlines.
Example: "Achieve a customer satisfaction rating of 90% or higher by the end of the fiscal year."

3. Achievable:
Ensure that the goal is realistic and attainable within the resources available (e.g., time, budget, skills). Set goals that stretch your abilities but are still possible to accomplish.
Example: "Complete the project within six months with the current team and budget constraints."

4. Relevant:
Align the goal with your overall objectives and priorities. It should be relevant to your long-term vision and contribute to organizational or personal growth.
Example: "Develop new product features that align with market trends and customer feedback."

5. Time-bound:
Set a specific timeframe or deadline for achieving the goal.

This creates a sense of urgency and helps prioritize tasks accordingly.

Example: "Launch the marketing campaign by the end of Q3 to capitalize on seasonal trends."

Benefits of SMART Goals:
- Clarity and Focus: Clearly defined goals provide direction and focus efforts toward achieving specific outcomes.
- Motivation and Accountability: Measurable criteria and deadlines motivate individuals or teams to work towards achieving the goal. It also facilitates accountability for results.
- Progress Tracking: Measurable criteria allow progress tracking, enabling adjustments to strategies or resource allocation as needed.
- Enhanced Decision Making: SMART goals help in prioritizing tasks and making informed decisions aligned with overarching objectives.

Implementing SMART Goals:
- Brainstorm and Define Goals: Collaborate with team members to brainstorm and define SMART goals that align with organizational objectives.
- Monitor Progress: Regularly monitor progress towards achieving SMART goals. Use performance metrics and milestones to assess success and make necessary adjustments.
- Celebrate Achievements: Celebrate milestones and achievements when SMART goals are accomplished. Recognize efforts and reinforce motivation for continued success.

By setting SMART goals, individuals and teams can effectively manage tasks and projects, maximize productivity, and achieve meaningful results aligned with organizational goals.

3.2. Tools for Project Management

Effective project management requires the use of tools and software to plan, organize, and track tasks and resources efficiently. Here are key tools commonly used for project management:

1. Trello:
- Description: Trello is a visual project management tool that uses boards, lists, and cards to organize tasks and workflows. It is highly flexible and allows teams to collaborate in real-time, assign tasks, set deadlines, and track progress easily.
- Features: Drag-and-drop interface, customizable boards, task assignments, due dates, checklists, attachments, comments, and integrations with other apps.

2. Asana:
- Description: Asana is a comprehensive project management platform designed to help teams coordinate and manage work effectively. It offers project tracking, task assignments, calendar views, and collaboration features.
- Features: Task lists, timelines, dependencies, project templates, file attachments, comments, notifications, reporting tools, and integrations with various apps and services.

3. Microsoft Project:
- Description: Microsoft Project is a powerful project management software that allows for detailed planning, scheduling, resource management, and tracking of projects. It is suitable for complex projects and large teams.
- Features: Gantt charts, task scheduling, resource allocation, budget tracking, collaboration tools, reporting capabilities, and integration with Microsoft Office suite.

4. Jira:
- Description: Jira is primarily used for agile project management, software development, and issue tracking. It offers customizable workflows, scrum boards, kanban boards, and advanced reporting capabilities.
- Features: User story mapping, sprint planning, backlog management, bug tracking, real-time collaboration, integration with development tools (e.g., GitHub, Bitbucket), and extensive plugin ecosystem.

5. Monday.com:
- Description: Monday.com is a versatile project management platform known for its visual and intuitive interface. It supports task management, project tracking, team collaboration, and workflow automation.
- Features: Customizable dashboards, timeline views, task dependencies, file sharing, communication tools, automations, integrations with third-party apps, and project analytics.

6. Basecamp:
- Description: Basecamp is a simple yet powerful project management and collaboration tool that centralizes project-related communication and tasks in one place. It is ideal for remote teams and small to medium-sized projects.
- Features: Project timelines, to-do lists, file storage, message boards, team chat, scheduling, client access, document collaboration, and automatic check-ins.

Choosing the Right Tool:
- Evaluate Needs: Consider the size of your team, project complexity, collaboration requirements, budget, and specific features needed (e.g., task management, time tracking, reporting).
- Trial and Feedback: Test different tools through trials or demos. Gather feedback from team members to assess

ease of use, effectiveness, and compatibility with existing workflows.
- Scalability: Ensure the selected tool can scale with your team and project requirements as they evolve over time.

Conclusion: Selecting the appropriate project management tool is crucial for organizing tasks, improving team collaboration, tracking progress, and ultimately achieving project success. Evaluate each tool's features and capabilities to determine the best fit for your organization's needs and project goals.

3.3. Effective Task Delegation

Effective task delegation is essential for optimizing team productivity and achieving project goals. Here are key strategies and best practices for successful task delegation:

1. Clear Communication:
- Clearly communicate task expectations, objectives, and deadlines to the team member(s) responsible for the task. Ensure mutual understanding of deliverables and desired outcomes.

2. Assess Team Skills and Strengths:
- Assign tasks to team members based on their skills, strengths, experience, and availability. Match tasks with individuals who have the expertise and resources necessary to complete them effectively.

3. Establish Accountability:
- Set clear expectations for accountability and ownership of delegated tasks. Define roles and responsibilities to ensure that team members understand their duties and are committed to achieving results.

4. Provide Adequate Resources:
- Equip team members with the necessary resources, tools, information, and support needed to accomplish delegated tasks successfully. Address any barriers or obstacles that may hinder progress.

5. Monitor Progress:
- Regularly monitor and track the progress of delegated tasks. Use project management tools or check-in meetings to assess milestones, address challenges, and provide guidance or feedback as needed.

- 6. Encourage Collaboration:
- Foster a collaborative environment where team members can seek assistance, share ideas, and collaborate on tasks when necessary. Encourage open communication and

teamwork to enhance productivity.

7. Empower Decision-Making:
- Delegate decision-making authority along with tasks whenever possible. Empower team members to make informed decisions within their delegated responsibilities, promoting autonomy and initiative.

8. Set Realistic Deadlines:
- Establish realistic and achievable deadlines for delegated tasks. Consider factors such as task complexity, dependencies, and resource availability when setting timelines to avoid overburdening team members.

9. Provide Feedback and Recognition:
- Offer constructive feedback on task performance to guide improvement and acknowledge accomplishments. Recognize and appreciate team members for their contributions and successful task completion.

10. Evaluate and Learn:
- Evaluate the outcomes of task delegation to identify strengths, areas for improvement, and lessons learned. Use insights to refine delegation strategies and enhance team efficiency over time.

Benefits of Effective Task Delegation:
- Improved Efficiency: Distributing tasks based on expertise and workload capacity increases efficiency and reduces workload imbalance.
- Enhanced Team Morale: Empowering team members through delegation promotes job satisfaction, skill development, and professional growth.
- Focus on Strategic Priorities: Leaders can prioritize strategic initiatives and high-value tasks by delegating operational and routine tasks effectively.
- Achievement of Goals: Successful task delegation aligns team efforts with organizational goals, driving overall project success and business outcomes.

By implementing these strategies for effective task delegation, project managers and team leaders can optimize team performance, foster collaboration, and achieve project objectives efficiently. Regular evaluation and adaptation of delegation practices ensure continuous improvement and sustained success in task management.

3.4. Effective Communication Strategies

Effective communication is crucial for successful task and project management. Here are key strategies to enhance communication within teams:

1. Clear and Concise Messages:
   Communicate information clearly and concisely to ensure understanding among team members. Use simple language and avoid ambiguity to convey messages effectively.

2. Active Listening:
   Practice active listening by paying attention to others' viewpoints, ideas, and concerns. Confirm understanding by paraphrasing and asking clarifying questions to promote clear communication.

3. Use of Communication Tools:
   Utilize appropriate communication tools and platforms (e.g., email, instant messaging, project management software) to facilitate timely and transparent communication. Choose tools that suit your team's preferences and needs.

4. Regular Updates and Progress Reports:
   Provide regular updates and progress reports to keep team members informed about project milestones, task status, and any changes in priorities. Scheduled meetings or status updates can help maintain alignment and accountability.

5. Foster Open Dialogue:
   Encourage open dialogue and constructive feedback within the team. Create a supportive environment where team members feel comfortable sharing ideas, raising concerns, and offering suggestions for improvement.

6. Clarify Roles and Responsibilities:
   Clearly define roles, responsibilities, and expectations for each team member. Ensure that everyone understands their tasks, deadlines, and how their work contributes to overall project goals.

7. Adapt Communication Styles:

Adapt communication styles to accommodate diverse preferences and personalities within the team. Flexibility in communication fosters understanding and collaboration among team members.

8. Address Conflict Proactively:

Address conflicts or misunderstandings promptly and constructively. Encourage open communication to resolve issues before they escalate, promoting a positive team dynamic and maintaining productivity.

9. Document Decisions and Action Items:

Document important decisions, action items, and meeting minutes to ensure clarity and accountability. Shared documentation helps mitigate misunderstandings and serves as a reference for future discussions.

10. Seek Feedback and Continuous Improvement:

Solicit feedback from team members on communication practices and processes. Continuously evaluate and refine communication strategies based on feedback to enhance team collaboration and project outcomes.

Effective communication strategies are essential for fostering collaboration, minimizing misunderstandings, and achieving project success. By implementing these strategies, teams can enhance productivity, maintain motivation, and effectively navigate challenges in task and project management.

MODULE 4:
LEADERSHIP AND TEAM MANAGEMENT

4.1. Leadership Styles

Effective leadership involves adopting various styles to inspire and guide teams toward achieving common goals. Here are key leadership styles commonly utilized in organizational settings:

1. Autocratic Leadership:
- Description: Autocratic leaders make decisions independently without consulting team members. They exercise strict control over tasks and processes, emphasizing efficiency and quick decision-making.
- Application: Suitable in situations requiring immediate decisions or in highly structured environments where clear direction is crucial (e.g., military operations, emergency response teams).

2. Democratic Leadership:
- Description: Democratic leaders involve team members in decision-making processes, encouraging participation, collaboration, and consensus-building. They value input from team members and foster a supportive work environment.
- Application: Effective in promoting innovation, creativity, and team engagement. It empowers team members to contribute ideas and solutions, enhancing morale and commitment.

3. Laissez-Faire Leadership:
- Description: Laissez-faire leaders delegate authority and decision-making to team members, providing minimal guidance or supervision. They trust team members' expertise and encourage autonomy in task execution.
- Application: Suitable for self-motivated and skilled teams capable of working independently. It fosters a sense of ownership and responsibility among team members, promoting initiative and innovation.

4. Transformational Leadership:

- Description: Transformational leaders inspire and motivate teams by articulating a compelling vision and encouraging commitment to organizational goals. They foster a culture of growth, continuous improvement, and shared success.
- Application: Effective in driving organizational change, fostering creativity, and empowering teams to achieve ambitious goals. Transformational leaders cultivate trust, loyalty, and a sense of purpose among team members.

5. Servant Leadership:

- Description: Servant leaders prioritize the needs of team members and strive to support their growth, development, and well-being. They lead by example, demonstrating humility, empathy, and a commitment to serving others.
- Application: Promotes a collaborative and inclusive work environment where team members feel valued and supported. Servant leaders empower individuals to reach their full potential and contribute to organizational success.

6. Transactional Leadership:

- Description: Transactional leaders emphasize clear roles, tasks, and expectations. They use rewards and punishments to motivate team members to achieve specific goals and adhere to established standards.
- Application: Effective in maintaining routine operations and ensuring compliance with organizational policies and procedures. Transactional leaders provide structure and accountability, driving performance and productivity.

Choosing the Right Leadership Style:

- Adaptability: Effective leaders understand when to apply different leadership styles based on situational demands, team dynamics, and organizational goals.

- **Flexibility:** Flexibility in leadership approach enables leaders to respond to challenges, capitalize on opportunities, and support team development effectively.
- **Continuous Improvement:** Reflecting on leadership effectiveness and seeking feedback from team members fosters growth and enhances leadership capabilities over time.

By leveraging appropriate leadership styles, leaders can cultivate a motivated and high-performing team, navigate challenges, and achieve sustainable success in their organizational roles.

4.2. Effective Team Building Strategies

Building and maintaining an effective team is essential for achieving organizational success. Here are key strategies for effective team building:

1. Clarify Team Goals and Objectives:
   Clearly define team goals, objectives, and expectations. Ensure that every team member understands their role in achieving these goals and how their contributions impact overall success.
2. Foster Open Communication:
   Encourage open and transparent communication within the team. Establish regular channels for sharing information, ideas, and feedback. Foster a supportive environment where team members feel comfortable expressing opinions and concerns.
3. Promote Collaboration and Trust:
   Foster a collaborative work environment where team members collaborate on tasks, share responsibilities, and leverage each other's strengths. Build trust among team members by promoting mutual respect, integrity, and reliability.
4. Encourage Diversity and Inclusion:
   Embrace diversity of perspectives, backgrounds, and skills within the team. Recognize and value different viewpoints and contributions. Foster inclusivity by creating opportunities for all team members to participate and contribute.
5. Provide Opportunities for Development:
   Support the professional and personal development of team members. Offer training, mentorship, and skill-building opportunities to enhance capabilities and promote career growth within the team.
6. Establish Clear Roles and Responsibilities:
   Define clear roles, responsibilities, and accountabilities for

each team member. Ensure alignment with team goals and avoid ambiguity to minimize misunderstandings and foster accountability.

7. Celebrate Achievements and Milestones:

Acknowledge and celebrate team achievements, milestones, and successes. Recognize individual and collective efforts to boost morale, motivation, and a sense of accomplishment within the team.

8. Manage Conflicts Effectively:

Address conflicts and disagreements promptly and constructively. Encourage open dialogue and active listening to understand different perspectives. Implement conflict resolution strategies to reach mutually beneficial resolutions.

9. Lead by Example:

Demonstrate leadership qualities by setting a positive example for the team. Display integrity, resilience, and a commitment to organizational values. Inspire and motivate team members through your actions and behaviors.

10. Evaluate and Adjust Strategies:

Continuously monitor team dynamics, performance, and effectiveness. Solicit feedback from team members and stakeholders to assess strategies and make necessary adjustments to improve team cohesion and productivity.

Benefits of Effective Team Building:
- Enhanced Productivity: Effective teams collaborate efficiently to achieve goals and deliver results.
- Improved Morale: A supportive and inclusive team environment fosters job satisfaction and engagement.
- Innovation and Creativity: Diverse perspectives and collaborative efforts lead to innovative solutions and continuous improvement.
- Stronger Organizational Culture: A cohesive team contributes to a positive organizational culture, attracting and retaining talent.

By implementing these effective team building strategies, leaders can cultivate a high-performing team capable of overcoming challenges, maximizing productivity, and achieving long-term success.

4.3. Effective Conflict Resolution Strategies

Conflict is inevitable in any team or organizational setting. Effective leaders utilize strategies to manage and resolve conflicts constructively. Here are key strategies for effective conflict resolution:

1. Address Issues Promptly:
Address conflicts promptly before they escalate. Encourage open communication and create a safe space for team members to express concerns and viewpoints.

2. Foster Understanding:
Promote empathy and understanding among team members. Encourage active listening and perspective-taking to grasp different viewpoints and underlying concerns.

3. Identify Root Causes:
Identify the root causes of conflicts rather than focusing solely on surface issues. Explore underlying reasons such as miscommunication, differing goals, or personality clashes.

4. Encourage Collaboration:
Encourage collaborative problem-solving. Facilitate discussions where conflicting parties work together to find mutually agreeable solutions and common ground.

5. Remain Neutral and Impartial:
Maintain neutrality and avoid taking sides in conflicts. Act as a mediator or facilitator to guide discussions toward resolution while respecting diverse perspectives.

6. Use Effective Communication Techniques:
Use clear and respectful communication techniques to de-escalate tensions. Encourage assertiveness without aggression and promote constructive dialogue.

7. Explore Compromise and Win-Win Solutions:
Explore compromise and win-win solutions where both parties feel their interests are acknowledged and respected. Seek outcomes that benefit the team and align with organizational goals.

8. Set Ground Rules and Norms:

Establish team norms and ground rules for resolving conflicts. Define acceptable behaviors and communication protocols to prevent misunderstandings and promote respect.

9. Seek Feedback and Follow-Up:

Solicit feedback from involved parties after conflict resolution to ensure satisfaction with outcomes. Follow up to monitor progress and address any lingering issues.

10. Learn from Conflicts:

View conflicts as opportunities for growth and learning. Reflect on conflict resolution processes to identify lessons learned and improve future conflict management strategies.

Benefits of Effective Conflict Resolution:
- Enhanced Team Cohesion: Resolving conflicts fosters trust, respect, and collaboration among team members.
- Improved Decision-Making: Constructive conflict resolution leads to better decision-making and innovative solutions.
- Positive Organizational Culture: Handling conflicts effectively contributes to a positive work environment and organizational culture.
- Reduced Stress and Turnover: Addressing conflicts promptly reduces stress and minimizes the risk of turnover within the team.

By implementing these effective conflict resolution strategies, leaders can mitigate conflicts, strengthen team relationships, and foster a supportive work environment conducive to productivity and growth.

4.4. Strategies for Motivating Teams

Motivating teams is crucial for enhancing productivity, morale, and overall performance. Effective leaders employ various strategies to inspire and energize their teams. Here are key strategies for motivating teams:

1. Set Clear Goals and Expectations:
Establish clear and achievable goals that align with organizational objectives. Ensure that team members understand their roles, responsibilities, and the importance of their contributions.

2. Provide Meaningful Feedback:
Offer regular feedback and recognition for individual and team achievements. Acknowledge progress, milestones, and efforts to reinforce positive behaviors and outcomes.

3. Foster a Positive Work Environment:
Cultivate a supportive and inclusive work environment where team members feel valued, respected, and motivated to contribute. Encourage camaraderie, teamwork, and open communication.

4. Offer Development Opportunities:
Provide opportunities for professional growth and skill development. Offer training, workshops, mentorship programs, and career advancement opportunities to empower team members and enhance their capabilities.

5. Encourage Autonomy and Empowerment:
Delegate responsibilities and decision-making authority to team members. Empower individuals to take ownership of their work, make decisions, and explore innovative solutions.

6. Celebrate Successes and Milestones:
Celebrate team successes, achievements, and milestones. Recognize individual and collective efforts through rewards, praise, team events, or public acknowledgments to boost morale and motivation.

7. Foster Collaboration and Teamwork:

Encourage collaboration and teamwork among team members. Promote a cooperative atmosphere where individuals support each other, share knowledge, and work together towards common goals.

8. Offer Rewards and Incentives:

Implement reward and incentive programs to motivate high performance. Consider monetary rewards, bonuses, extra time off, or other incentives that align with team goals and individual preferences.

9. Lead by Example:

Demonstrate leadership qualities and behaviors that inspire others. Display enthusiasm, dedication, and a commitment to excellence in your own work to set a positive example for the team.

10. Solicit Feedback and Adapt Strategies:

Seek input from team members on motivational strategies and initiatives. Continuously evaluate and adapt motivational approaches based on feedback and evolving team dynamics.

Benefits of Motivating Teams:
- Increased Productivity: Motivated teams are more productive and committed to achieving goals.
- Enhanced Job Satisfaction: Higher morale and job satisfaction lead to greater employee retention and loyalty.
- Innovation and Creativity: Motivated teams are more likely to generate innovative ideas and solutions.
- Improved Organizational Performance: Motivated teams contribute to overall organizational success and competitiveness in the marketplace.

By implementing these strategies for motivating teams, leaders can create a positive and high-performing work environment where team members are motivated, engaged, and inspired to achieve their best.

MODULE 5:
PERSONAL DEVELOPMENT AND GROWTH

5.1. Importance of Continuous Learning

Continuous learning plays a crucial role in personal and professional development, enabling individuals to adapt to changes, acquire new skills, and achieve career growth. Here are key reasons highlighting the importance of continuous learning:

1. Skill Enhancement:

Continuous learning allows individuals to continuously upgrade their skills and knowledge in their field of expertise. It enables them to stay relevant in a rapidly evolving job market and meet the demands of new technologies and practices.

2. Adaptability:

Learning new skills and knowledge enhances adaptability to changing work environments and industry trends. It equips individuals with the flexibility to take on new roles, responsibilities, and challenges effectively.

3. Career Advancement:

Continuous learning enhances career prospects by opening up opportunities for promotions, job transitions, and professional growth. It demonstrates a commitment to self-improvement and increases confidence in tackling higher-level responsibilities.

4. Innovation and Problem-Solving:

Acquiring new knowledge and perspectives stimulates innovation and creativity. It enables individuals to approach problems from different angles, propose innovative solutions, and contribute to organizational success.

5. Personal Fulfillment:

Learning fosters personal satisfaction and fulfillment by pursuing interests, passions, and intellectual curiosity. It provides a sense of accomplishment and self-confidence as individuals achieve their learning goals.

6. Networking and Collaboration:

Engaging in continuous learning facilitates networking opportunities and collaboration with like-minded professionals. It expands professional connections, fosters knowledge sharing, and promotes career development through mentorship and peer support.

7. Stay Updated with Industry Trends:

Continuous learning ensures individuals remain updated with the latest industry trends, best practices, and regulations. It positions them as informed and knowledgeable contributors within their organization and industry.

8. Adapt to Technological Advances:

Rapid technological advancements require continuous learning to navigate new tools, software, and digital platforms effectively. Embracing technology through learning enhances productivity and efficiency in work processes.

9. Personal and Professional Growth:

Continuous learning contributes to holistic personal and professional growth. It cultivates critical thinking, problem-solving skills, leadership abilities, and resilience, preparing individuals for diverse challenges and opportunities.

10. Cultivate a Learning Culture:

Promoting a culture of continuous learning within organizations encourages lifelong learning among employees. It fosters a supportive environment where learning is valued, encouraged, and integrated into daily practices.

Benefits of Continuous Learning:
- Enhanced Job Performance: Continuous learners demonstrate improved job performance and contribute effectively to organizational goals.

- Career Resilience: Acquiring diverse skills and knowledge enhances career resilience and adaptability to industry changes.
- Professional Recognition: Continuous learners are recognized for their expertise, credibility, and leadership in their respective fields.
- Personal Growth: Learning fosters personal development, self-confidence, and a sense of purpose in professional endeavors.

By prioritizing continuous learning, individuals can proactively invest in their development, remain competitive in their careers, and contribute positively to organizational success and innovation.

5.2. Strategies for Effective Time Management

Effective time management is essential for maximizing productivity, achieving goals, and maintaining work-life balance. Here are key strategies to improve time management skills:

1. Prioritize Tasks:

Identify and prioritize tasks based on urgency and importance. Use techniques like Eisenhower Matrix (urgent vs. important) to categorize tasks and allocate time accordingly.

2. Set SMART Goals:

Establish Specific, Measurable, Achievable, Relevant, and Time-bound (SMART) goals. Break down larger goals into smaller, manageable tasks with clear deadlines to maintain focus and track progress.

3. Create a Daily Schedule:

Plan and organize daily activities using a schedule or planner. Allocate dedicated time slots for tasks, meetings, breaks, and personal activities to optimize productivity and minimize procrastination.

4. Minimize Distractions:

Identify and minimize distractions that can disrupt workflow. Implement strategies such as setting boundaries, turning off notifications, and creating a conducive work environment to maintain concentration.

5. Use Time Management Tools:

Utilize technology and productivity tools (e.g., calendars, task management apps, time tracking software) to organize tasks, set reminders, and prioritize activities. Leverage tools that align with your preferred working style and needs.

6. Practice Time Blocking:

Allocate specific time blocks for focused work on tasks or projects. Dedicate uninterrupted periods for deep work to enhance concentration and productivity without interruptions.

7. Delegate Tasks:

Delegate tasks to team members or collaborate with others when appropriate. Assign tasks based on strengths and expertise, allowing you to focus on high-priority activities and strategic initiatives.

8. Learn to Say No:

Prioritize your workload by politely declining tasks or commitments that do not align with your goals or current priorities. Saying no helps preserve time and energy for tasks that contribute to your success.

9. Review and Adjust:

Regularly review your time management strategies and adjust them based on changing priorities, workload, and personal preferences. Continuously evaluate effectiveness and make necessary improvements.

10. Practice Self-Care:

Maintain a healthy work-life balance by incorporating self-care activities into your schedule. Prioritize rest, exercise, and relaxation to recharge and sustain productivity over the long term.

Benefits of Effective Time Management:
- Increased Productivity: Efficient use of time leads to higher productivity and accomplishment of tasks.
- Reduced Stress: Effective time management minimizes stress and prevents burnout by managing workload and deadlines effectively.
- Improved Decision-Making: Clear priorities and organized schedules facilitate better decision-making and problem-solving abilities.
- Achievement of Goals: Structured time management enables individuals to achieve personal and professional goals more effectively.

By implementing these strategies for effective time management, individuals can optimize their productivity, maintain work-life balance, and achieve success in their personal and professional endeavors.

5.3. Strategies for Effective Stress Management

Effective stress management is essential for maintaining well-being and productivity. Here are key strategies to manage stress effectively:

1. Identify Stress Triggers:
   Recognize and understand the sources of stress in your life. Identify specific situations, tasks, or interactions that contribute to feelings of stress and anxiety.
2. Practice Relaxation Techniques:
   Incorporate relaxation techniques into your daily routine. Techniques such as deep breathing, meditation, yoga, or progressive muscle relaxation can help reduce stress levels and promote calmness.
3. Exercise Regularly:
   Engage in regular physical activity to alleviate stress and boost mood. Exercise releases endorphins, which are natural stress relievers, and improves overall physical and mental well-being.
4. Maintain a Healthy Lifestyle:
   Adopt a balanced diet, adequate sleep, and hydration to support your body's ability to cope with stress. Avoid excessive caffeine, alcohol, and unhealthy coping mechanisms.
5. Establish Boundaries:
   Set boundaries to protect your time and energy. Learn to say no to additional responsibilities or commitments that may contribute to stress overload.
6. Prioritize Tasks and Time Management:
   Use effective time management techniques to prioritize tasks and reduce feelings of overwhelm. Break down tasks into smaller, manageable steps and allocate time for each task accordingly.

7. Seek Social Support:
Connect with supportive friends, family members, or colleagues who can offer encouragement, advice, and perspective during stressful times. Sharing experiences and feelings can provide emotional relief.

8. Practice Mindfulness:
Cultivate mindfulness through practices such as mindfulness meditation or mindfulness-based stress reduction (MBSR). Mindfulness helps you stay present, manage negative thoughts, and reduce stress reactivity.

9. Learn Stress-Reduction Techniques:
Explore and learn stress-reduction techniques such as cognitive behavioral therapy (CBT), biofeedback, or relaxation response techniques to manage stress effectively.

10. Take Breaks and Disconnect:
Schedule regular breaks throughout the day to rest and recharge. Disconnect from work or digital devices during breaks to promote relaxation and prevent burnout.

Benefits of Effective Stress Management:
- Improved Health: Reduced stress levels contribute to better physical and mental health outcomes.
- Enhanced Productivity: Managing stress improves focus, concentration, and productivity at work and in daily activities.
- Better Relationships: Reduced stress promotes healthier relationships and communication with others.
- Increased Resilience: Effective stress management builds resilience to cope with challenges and setbacks.

By implementing these strategies for effective stress management, individuals can enhance their overall well-being, maintain resilience, and achieve a healthier work-life balance.

5.4. Strategies for Enhancing Emotional Intelligence

Emotional intelligence (EI) plays a critical role in personal and professional success by influencing self-awareness, self-management, social awareness, and relationship management. Here are key strategies to enhance emotional intelligence:

1. Develop Self-Awareness:
Increase awareness of your emotions, thoughts, and reactions. Practice mindfulness and reflection to recognize emotional triggers and understand how they influence your behavior.

2. Manage Emotions Effectively:
Learn to regulate and manage your emotions in challenging situations. Utilize techniques such as deep breathing, positive self-talk, and stress management to maintain emotional balance.

3. Cultivate Empathy:
Enhance empathy by actively listening to others, seeking to understand their perspectives, and recognizing their emotions. Put yourself in others' shoes to foster deeper connections and empathy.

4. Improve Social Skills:
Develop effective communication skills, conflict resolution techniques, and teamwork abilities. Build rapport, adapt communication styles, and collaborate effectively with diverse groups.

5. Practice Assertiveness:
Assert your needs, opinions, and boundaries while respecting the rights and perspectives of others. Communicate assertively to express yourself clearly and confidently without aggression.

6. Enhance Self-Motivation:
Set meaningful goals, maintain optimism, and persevere in

the face of setbacks. Cultivate a growth mindset and focus on intrinsic motivation to achieve personal and professional aspirations.

7. Develop Resilience:

Build resilience to cope with stress, adversity, and change. Embrace challenges as opportunities for growth, learn from setbacks, and bounce back stronger with adaptive coping strategies.

8. Foster Positive Relationships:

Nurture supportive and positive relationships with colleagues, friends, and family members. Build trust, respect, and open communication to cultivate a supportive network.

9. Seek Feedback and Learn from Experiences:

Solicit constructive feedback to gain insights into your strengths and areas for improvement. Reflect on experiences, learn from mistakes, and apply lessons learned to enhance emotional intelligence.

10. Practice Mindful Decision-Making:

Make thoughtful and mindful decisions by considering emotions, facts, and potential outcomes. Evaluate decisions from multiple perspectives and choose actions aligned with your values and goals.

Benefits of Enhancing Emotional Intelligence:
- Improved Relationships: Stronger interpersonal connections and effective communication.
- Enhanced Leadership Skills: Effective leadership, influence, and decision-making capabilities.
- Increased Self-Awareness: Greater understanding of strengths, weaknesses, and personal development areas.
- Better Stress Management: Improved resilience and ability to handle stress effectively.

By prioritizing the development of emotional intelligence

through these strategies, individuals can enhance their personal growth, professional success, and overall well-being.

MODULE 6:
CAREER DEVELOPMENT

6.1. Setting Career Goals

Setting clear and achievable career goals is essential for guiding your professional growth and development. Here are key steps and considerations for setting effective career goals:

1. Self-Assessment:
Reflect on your interests, strengths, values, and skills. Assess your current job satisfaction and career trajectory to identify areas for improvement or change.

2. Define Your Objectives:
Clarify what you want to achieve in your career. Set specific and measurable goals that align with your long-term aspirations, such as acquiring new skills, advancing in your current role, or transitioning to a new industry.

3. Prioritize Goals:
Rank your goals based on their importance and relevance to your overall career strategy. Focus on goals that will have the greatest impact on your professional growth and job satisfaction.

4. Set SMART Goals:
Ensure your goals are Specific, Measurable, Achievable, Relevant, and Time-bound (SMART). Break down larger goals into smaller, actionable steps with clear deadlines to track progress effectively.

5. Create an Action Plan:
Develop a detailed action plan outlining the steps required to achieve each goal. Identify resources, skills, and support needed to overcome potential obstacles and achieve success.

6. Seek Feedback and Advice:
Consult with mentors, career advisors, or trusted colleagues to gain insights and feedback on your career goals. Incorporate constructive feedback to refine your goals and action plan.

7. Stay Flexible and Adapt:

Remain open to adjusting your goals and plans based on changing circumstances, opportunities, and personal growth. Embrace learning experiences and unexpected opportunities that align with your career aspirations.

8. Monitor Progress:

Regularly review your progress towards achieving your career goals. Track milestones, celebrate achievements, and assess challenges to stay motivated and focused on continuous improvement.

9. Develop Skills and Knowledge:

Invest in professional development opportunities to enhance your skills and knowledge relevant to your career goals. Attend workshops, courses, or seminars to stay competitive in your field.

10. Evaluate and Revise Goals as Needed:

Periodically evaluate your career goals and revise them as necessary to reflect changes in priorities, interests, or career opportunities. Continuously strive for alignment with your evolving aspirations.

Benefits of Setting Career Goals:
- Direction and Focus: Clear goals provide direction and focus in your career journey.
- Motivation and Accountability: Goals motivate you to take action and hold yourself accountable for your professional development.
- Achievement and Satisfaction: Accomplishing goals leads to a sense of achievement and fulfillment in your career.
- Career Growth: Setting and achieving goals facilitates career advancement and opportunities for personal and professional growth.

By setting clear and meaningful career goals using these

strategies, you can navigate your career path effectively, maximize opportunities, and achieve long-term success in your chosen field.

6.2. Developing Professional Skills

Developing professional skills is essential for advancing in your career and achieving long-term success. Here are key strategies to enhance your professional skills:

1. Identify Relevant Skills:
Identify the skills required in your current role or desired career path. Research industry trends and job descriptions to determine which skills are most valued and relevant.

2. Set Learning Goals:
Set specific learning goals to acquire or improve upon targeted skills. Prioritize skills that align with your career aspirations and will contribute to your professional development.

3. Seek Learning Opportunities:
Pursue formal education, certifications, workshops, or online courses to develop new skills. Take advantage of training programs offered by your employer or professional associations.

4. Practice Continual Learning:
Embrace a mindset of continual learning and improvement. Stay updated with industry developments, best practices, and emerging trends through reading, networking, and attending conferences.

5. Apply Skills in Real-World Scenarios:
Apply newly acquired skills in practical situations to gain hands-on experience and deepen your understanding. Seek opportunities within your current role or through volunteer work and projects.

6. Receive Feedback and Mentorship:
Seek feedback from supervisors, mentors, or peers on your skill development progress. Use constructive feedback to refine your skills and identify areas for further improvement.

7. Develop Soft Skills:

Enhance soft skills such as communication, teamwork, leadership, and problem-solving. These skills are critical for effective collaboration, relationship-building, and career advancement.

8. Utilize Technology and Tools:

Familiarize yourself with relevant technology, tools, and software applications in your field. Stay proficient in digital literacy to adapt to technological advancements and streamline work processes.

9. Network and Collaborate:

Engage with professionals in your industry through networking events, professional associations, and online communities. Collaborate on projects or participate in mentorship programs to expand your skills and knowledge.

10. Evaluate Progress and Set New Goals:

Regularly assess your skill development progress against your learning goals. Reflect on achievements, challenges, and areas for growth to set new goals and continue advancing professionally.

Benefits of Developing Professional Skills:
- Career Advancement: Enhanced skills increase your competitiveness and eligibility for promotions and career opportunities.
- Personal Growth: Continuous skill development fosters personal satisfaction, confidence, and professional fulfillment.
- Adaptability: Acquiring diverse skills enhances your ability to adapt to changing job roles, industry demands, and technological advancements.
- Job Satisfaction: Mastery of skills contributes to job satisfaction by enabling you to perform tasks effectively and contribute meaningfully to organizational goals.

By focusing on developing and enhancing your professional skills using these strategies, you can strengthen your career foundation, expand your opportunities, and achieve your professional aspirations.

6.3. Building Effective Networking Skills

Effective networking is crucial for career advancement and professional success. Here are key strategies to build and improve your networking skills:

1. Define Your Networking Goals:

Clarify your objectives for networking, such as expanding your professional contacts, seeking career advice, or exploring new opportunities. Set specific goals to guide your networking efforts.

2. Attend Networking Events:

Participate in industry conferences, seminars, workshops, and networking events. Actively engage with professionals from diverse backgrounds to broaden your network and exchange insights.

3. Develop a Professional Online Presence:

Create and maintain profiles on professional networking platforms such as LinkedIn. Showcase your skills, experiences, and career interests to connect with like-minded professionals and potential employers.

4. Cultivate Genuine Relationships:

Build authentic relationships based on mutual respect and trust. Listen actively, show interest in others' perspectives, and offer support or assistance when possible to foster meaningful connections.

5. Practice Effective Communication:

Master the art of clear and concise communication. Prepare an elevator pitch to introduce yourself professionally and articulate your career goals, achievements, and areas of expertise.

6. Follow Up and Stay Connected:

Follow up with contacts after networking events or meetings. Send personalized messages expressing appreciation and continue to nurture relationships through regular communication and updates.

7. Offer Value and Be Generous:

Be willing to share knowledge, insights, and resources with your network. Offer assistance, make introductions, and provide support to demonstrate your value as a trusted and reliable connection.

8. Seek Mentorship and Guidance:

Seek mentorship from experienced professionals or peers within your network. Build relationships with mentors who can offer guidance, career advice, and constructive feedback on your professional development.

9. Attend Industry Association Meetings:

Join and actively participate in industry-specific associations or professional groups. Attend meetings, contribute to discussions, and collaborate on initiatives to establish credibility and expand your network.

10. Maintain Professionalism and Integrity:

Uphold professional ethics, integrity, and confidentiality in all networking interactions. Respect others' privacy and boundaries while maintaining a positive and professional demeanor.

Benefits of Effective Networking:
- Career Opportunities: Networking enhances visibility and access to job openings, referrals, and career opportunities.
- Knowledge and Insights: Access to diverse perspectives, industry trends, and valuable insights shared within your network.
- Personal and Professional Growth: Networking fosters personal development, confidence, and continuous learning through exposure to new ideas and experiences.
- Support and Collaboration: Build a supportive network of peers, mentors, and collaborators who can offer advice, encouragement, and collaborative opportunities.

By actively developing and honing your networking skills using these strategies, you can expand your professional connections, leverage opportunities for career advancement, and achieve long-term success in your chosen field.

ADDITIONAL MATERIALS

Networking Skills Development Checklist

1. Define Your Networking Goals:
Clarify objectives for networking (e.g., career advice, job opportunities, industry insights).

2. Attend Networking Events:
Participate in industry conferences, seminars, and networking meetups.

3. Maintain Online Presence:
Create/update LinkedIn profile; showcase skills, experiences, and career interests.

4. Build Authentic Relationships:
Cultivate genuine connections based on mutual respect and trust.

5. Practice Effective Communication:
Prepare and practice an elevator pitch; communicate goals and achievements clearly.

6. Follow Up and Stay Connected:
Send personalized follow-up messages after networking events; stay in touch regularly.

7. Offer Value to Your Network:
Share knowledge, make introductions, and provide assistance to contacts.

8. Seek Mentorship:
Identify and connect with mentors who can offer guidance and career advice.

9. Attend Industry Meetings:
Join industry associations; attend meetings and contribute to discussions.

10. Maintain Professionalism:
Uphold ethical standards and respect confidentiality in all networking interactions.

11. Reflect and Adapt:
Regularly assess networking efforts; adjust strategies based

on feedback and experiences.

12. Expand and Diversify Connections:

Reach out to professionals from diverse backgrounds and industries.

13. Stay Informed:

Stay updated on industry trends, news, and developments relevant to your network.

14. Practice Patience and Persistence:

Networking takes time; be patient and persistent in building meaningful connections.

15. Evaluate Networking ROI:

Measure success in achieving networking goals; track career opportunities and insights gained.

Using this checklist can help you systematically enhance your networking skills, build a strong professional network, and leverage opportunities for career growth and development.

Recommended Books

- "Never Eat Alone: And Other Secrets to Success, One Relationship at a Time" by Keith Ferrazzi and Tahl Raz

This book emphasizes the importance of building and maintaining relationships for career success and personal growth.

- "How to Win Friends and Influence People" by Dale Carnegie

A classic on interpersonal skills, offering timeless advice on building rapport, communication, and influencing others.

- "The Start-Up of You: Adapt to the Future, Invest in Yourself, and Transform Your Career" by Reid Hoffman and Ben Casnocha

Focuses on strategies for networking and managing your career as if it were a start-up.

- "Give and Take: Why Helping Others Drives Our Success" by Adam Grant

Explores the benefits of networking and building relationships based on generosity and giving.

- "Networking Like a Pro: Turning Contacts into Connections" by Ivan Misner, David Alexander, and Brian Hilliard

Provides practical tips and strategies for effective networking in both personal and professional settings.

- "The Power of Who: You Already Know Everyone You Need to Know" by Bob Beaudine

Emphasizes leveraging existing relationships and connections to achieve career and personal goals.

- "The Charisma Myth: How Anyone Can Master the Art and Science of Personal Magnetism" by Olivia Fox Cabane

Offers insights into developing personal charisma and enhancing interpersonal relationships.

- "Radical Candor: Be a Kick-Ass Boss Without Losing Your Humanity" by Kim Scott

Focuses on building strong professional relationships through honest and constructive communication.

- "Connected: The Surprising Power of Our Social Networks and How They Shape Our Lives" by Nicholas A. Christakis and James H. Fowler

Explores the impact of social networks on personal and professional success, providing insights into how connections influence our lives.

- "The Art of Work: A Proven Path to Discovering What You Were Meant to Do" by Jeff Goins

While not solely focused on networking, it offers guidance on finding meaningful work through relationships and connections.

These books cover various aspects of networking, from building relationships to leveraging connections for career advancement and personal growth. Each offers unique perspectives and actionable advice to help you enhance your networking skills effectively.

Parting words

Congratulations on completing the course on Enhancing Personal and Professional Productivity! Throughout this journey, you have explored essential strategies and techniques to maximize your efficiency, achieve your goals, and lead a more productive life.

Remember, productivity is not just about managing time; it's about making deliberate choices, prioritizing effectively, and continuously improving your workflow. By applying the principles learned in this course—whether it's setting SMART goals, adopting productivity tools, or cultivating a growth mindset—you are equipped to navigate challenges and seize opportunities in your personal and professional endeavors.

As you move forward, continue to refine your skills, embrace new learning opportunities, and adapt to changes in your environment. Stay committed to your goals, maintain a healthy work-life balance, and leverage your newfound knowledge to drive meaningful outcomes.

Thank you for your dedication and participation. Here's to your continued success in enhancing your personal and professional productivity!

Course: Enhancing Personal and Professional Productivity - Benshi

NOTES

NOTES

Course: Enhancing Personal and Professional Productivity - Benshi

NOTES

Course: Enhancing Personal and Professional Productivity - Benshi

NOTES

NOTES

Course: Enhancing Personal and Professional Productivity - Benshi

NOTES

Course: Enhancing Personal and Professional Productivity - Benshi

NOTES

Course: Enhancing Personal and Professional Productivity - Benshi

NOTES

www.ingramcontent.com/pod-product-compliance
Lightning Source LLC
Chambersburg PA
CBHW071840210526
45479CB00001B/222